NATIONAL SECURITY AGENCY
Ft. George G. Meade, MD

Serial: I732-001R-2010
28 April 2010

Network Infrastructure Division
Systems and Network Analysis Center

Activating Authentication and Encryption for Cisco Unified Communications Manager Express (CUCME) 7.0/4.3

This document
contains 30 sheets.

Table of Contents

Executive Summary

The intent of this document is to provide step-by-step instructions for configuring authentication and encryption for Cisco Unified Communications Manager Express (CUCME) releases 4.2, and 7.0/4.3. These procedures will provide a higher level of CUCME security, including the following features:

- Voice media encryption using Secure Real-Time Transport Protocol (SRTP)
- Authentication between the CUCME and the phones
- Encryption of the call signaling between the CUCME and the phones
- Authentication of Trivial File Transfer Protocol (TFTP) files

Although, Cisco has a very comprehensive document covering this topic, it is hard to follow and some steps are not in the right order. This document is an explanation of Cisco's CUCME security guide. This document will provide high-level system requirements and restrictions on the capabilities of the CUCME. Also included are the instructions for configuring the Certificate Trust List (CTL), Certificate Authority Proxy Function (CAPF) Service, Certificate Authority (CA), phone security mode, and hardening the phone.

1 Introduction and Security Overview

When Voice over Internet Protocol (VoIP) users are asked about security concerns related to VoIP, one of the first thoughts is how to secure the VoIP network itself. Although, applying security measures at Layer 2 through Layer 5 (switches, routers, firewalls, and Intrusion Detection Systems) are important and necessary, these steps do not fully encompass a Defense in Depth strategy. To take full advantage of Defense in Depth countermeasures, media encryption at the presentation layer (Layer 6) must also be implemented.

To set a baseline for understanding authentication and encryption, basic terminologies need to be understood. This section will provide an understanding of why authentication and encryption is important. The terminologies used throughout the document are further defined in Appendix A. The use of authentication and encryption will protect confidentiality and make it harder for individuals (internal and external) from tampering with the signaling and media streams, the CUCME router, and IP phones. The NSA Information Assurance Directorate's (IAD) guidance provided in the "Security Guidance for Deploying IP Telephony Systems" document, states that authentication and encryption services should be activated on any VoIP network and associated IP phones. When the security features are activated, the media streams and call signaling between Cisco IP phones are encrypted, the files sent between the CUCME and the phones are digitally signed, and the network communication streams are authenticated.

The procedures in this document are designed for individuals familiar with Cisco's IOS and the command line interface used to configure Cisco devices. It is also assumed that the CUCME is already configured and operational without security installed. This document only serves to explain the procedures of implementing authentication and security on the CUCME.

2 System Requirements and Restrictions

In order to activate the authentication and encryption on CUCME, the following system requirements and restrictions must be considered:

Requirements:

- CUCME phone authentication requires the Cisco IOS feature set Advanced Enterprise Services (adventerprisek9) or Advanced IP Services (advipservicesk9) on supported platforms. Currently the supported platforms included the 2800, 2900, 3200, 3800, and 3900 series routers.
- CUCME 4.2 or later is require to provide media encryption

Restrictions and Interactions:

- Media and signaling encryption will not function if the Cisco CTL client service is not activated and installed on the CUCME router.
- Secure three-way software conference is not supported.

- If a party drops from a three-party conference, the call between the remaining two parties returns to a secure state if the two endpoints are configured for encryption.
- Calls to Cisco Unity Express are not secure.
- Music on Hold (MOH) is not secure.
- Modem relay and T.3 fax relay calls are not secure.
- Media flow-around is not supported for call transfer and call forward.
- Secure Cisco CUCME does not support Session Initiation Protocol (SIP) trunks; only H.323 trunks are supported.

Notes: Listed above are primary restrictions, interactions, and requirements. Detailed listing of all requirements, restrictions, and interactions, refers to the Configuring Security section of the Cisco Unified Communications Manager Express Administration Guide at:
http://www.cisco.com/en/US/docs/voice_ip_comm/cucme/admin/configuration/guide/cmead.pdf.

3 Configuring Authentication and Encryption

There are several steps involved in configuring authentication and encryption. These steps include configuring a CA, the CAPF server, the CTL client, and creating certificates with the CA. After completing those tasks, authentication and encryption can be enabled. Last, all the devices that are connected to the CUCME must be hardened to provide the highest level of assurance.

3.1 Configuring the IOS Certificate Authority

Enabling encryption and authentication on the CUCME requires the use of a CA. The CA can be configured on the CUCME router as shown below or it can be a third party CA. The CA that is created will be used to enroll certificates for each of the various CUCME server functions. The server functions that require a certificate include the CUCME server and the CAPF server. Two additional certificates must be enrolled with the CA to take the place of the Site Administrator Security Token (SAST) tokens that are used by the CTL client. The SAST tokens that are used by a full sized CUCM will not operate on a Cisco router, and are not required for CUCME to operate securely.

The following commands are required to configure the IOS CA. The first step towards configuring the CA is to enter the "enable" mode and type "config t" to begin the configuration. Once in the global configuration mode enter the following commands:

```
ip http server
crypto pki server <Name of the CA server>
 database level {minimal | names | complete}
 database url flash:
 grant auto
 exit
```

HTTP Sever: The HTTP server is normally turned off for security reasons, but is required to authenticate and enroll the certificates that are created by the router. Access Control Lists (ACLs) can be applied to block this port on all interfaces if desired. If the HTTP server is disabled then the certificates can no longer be validated and all phones will lose their connection with the CUCME. Since this does create a security risk, it is suggested that a third party CA be used to eliminate the use of the HTTP server on the router.

Database configuration: The "crypto pki server" command creates a CA server on the IOS with the name that was provided. The next two commands specify how much information is stored in the certificate enrollment database, and the location of the database. The example shown in Appendix B will store all of the certificates and enrollment database information on the flash memory. For the purpose of securing the CUCME, this is sufficient. If the CA is used for other purposes, then the database may not fit on the flash and it may need to be moved, less information be stored, or a larger flash card be installed. The database location Universal Resource Locator (URL) can be set to any URL that is supported by the Cisco IOS file system. These supported URLs include TFTP, flash, and NVRAM.

"grant auto": Before the CA will allow any certificates to be enrolled, the "grant" command must be entered. There are different methods of granting enrollment. The first and easiest method is shown above with the "auto" parameter. This will allow all certificates to be accepted and enrolled into the CA. Other methods require additional information, but still provide the means for auto enrollment. It is recommended that if this option is used, that it is only used during the setup and configuration phase. Once the different server certificates and phone certificates are enrolled, the "grant auto" command should be turned off. However the "grant auto" must be enabled for updates to any of the certificates.

The following set of commands demonstrates how to configure the CA's trust point and enable the CA.

```
crypto pki trustpoint <Name of the CA server>
 enrollment url http://<IP address of CUCME>:80
 exit
crypto pki server <Name of the CA server>
 no shutdown
 exit
```

"enrollment": When creating the CA server, a trust point will be created automatically. In addition, this trust point will become the CA root certificate. The problem with the automatic creation of this certificate is that there is no means to use the certificate to enroll with the CA. The CAPF server that will be shown later in this document requires the CA server's certificate to enroll the phone certificates. For this reason, the CA server trust point must be configured with an enrollment URL before activating the CA. The URL that is used in this command should be the location of the CA, which is the IP address of the CUCME.

"no shutdown": The CA is disabled by default and will not begin until the "no shutdown" command is issued. When this command is entered, the CA will become active and will prompt the user for a password to be assigned. This password is used later in the configuration and should comply with the organization's security policy.

At this point in the configuration, the CA should be configured and running. To verify that the configuration is correct, the running configuration should contain entries similar to the following:

```
ip http server
!
crypto pki server CAserver
 database level complete
 grant auto
 database url flash:/
!
crypto pki trustpoint CAserver
 enrollment url http://3.3.3.1:80
 revocation-check crl
 rsakeypair CAserver
```

Notice that there is a trust point for the CA server created automatically. This trust point can be used to change the size of the RSA keys or how the CA server's certificate is enrolled. The items that are shown in bold type are labels or IP addresses that can be changed, and are specific to the administrator's implementation.

3.2   Creating Certificates for Server Functions

Before any of the additional server functions can be installed, a certificate must be received from the CA. These certificates are received from the CA by creating a trust point and enrolling it with the CA. Cisco uses the term trust point in the IOS configuration. In other words, a trust point is a way to associate a name to a certificate generated by the CA.

Several of the CUCME server functions can be configured with their own trust points. Another option is for the majority of the server functions to share a single trust point. The server functions that can share a trust point are the CUCME, the TFTP, and CAPF servers. The following commands, shown in sections 3.2.1 and 3.2.2, can be entered when in the configuration mode for creating the two trust points. For the highest level of security and best practices, each server function should be assigned separate certificates. For the purposes of this paper, the different server functions will share a trust point. To create a separate trust point for each server function, the procedures that are described in section 3.2.1 must be repeated as needed.

The first trust point that is created will be used for the CUCME, TFTP, CAPF servers, and the first System Administrator Security Token (SAST). An additional trust point is required for the second SAST that will be used as the backup for the

CTL-client. The CTL file is a requirement for each of the phones; without the backup trust point, the CTL file will not be created.

3.2.1 Creating a Certificate for CUCME, TFTP, CAPF, and SAST1 Servers

The following commands are required to generate the certificate for the CUCME, TFTP, CAPF, and the first SAST. The first step to generating the required certificate is to enter "enable" mode and enter "config t" to begin configuration. Once in the configuration mode enter the following commands:

```
crypto pki trustpoint <CUCME servers' trustpoint>
 enrollment url http://<IP address of CUCME>:80
 revocation-check method1 [method2 [method3]]
 rsakeypair <key-label> [key-size[encryption-key-size]]
 exit
```

"crypto pki trustpoint": The "crypto pki trustpoint" command creates a new trust point with a given name and enters the configuration of that trust point. The trust point that is being created with this series of commands will be used for the CUCME, TFTP, CAPF, and one of the certificates required for the CTL-client known as SAST1.

"enrollment": The "enrollment" command tells the trust point which CA to register with. In this example the CUCME router has it's own CA and enrolls with itself. If this were a third party CA then the URL for that CA would be used.

"revocation-check": Certificate revocation becomes an issue when using a Public Key Infrastructure (PKI), therefore this is addressed in the trust point. The revocation checking can be performed using either a Certificate Revocation List (CRL) or the Online Certificate Status Protocol (OCSP). In the "revocation-check" command, the valid options include "none", "crl", or "ocsp". It is recommended that some kind of certificate revocation is performed, and therefore the option "none" should not be used.

"rsakeypair": The last command shown here states the label and size of the RSA key pair that will be associated with this trust point. Valid key sizes include 512, 1024, and 2048. A key size of 1024 is recommended, because it provides adequate security and some phones may not support the larger 2048 size keys.

The next step to creating the certificate is to authenticate and enroll the trust point with the CA. The following set of commands will perform the authentication and enrollment of the CUCME servers' trust point with the IOS CA. Each of these commands will provide interactive prompts. The responses to these prompts will be decided based upon the user's security policies. These prompts include how much and what information will be displayed in the public certificates. Also a prompt will be provided for the certificate revocation password.

```
crypto pki authenticate <CUCME servers' trustpoint>
```

```
crypto pki enroll <CUCME servers' trustpoint>
```

This completes the creation of the certificate that will be used by the CUCME, CAPF, and TFTP servers. If separate certificates are being created for each server then repeat as necessary. The CTL-client will also use this certificate as its primary certificate. The router configuration should now contain entries similar to the ones below.

```
crypto pki trustpoint CUCME_CAPF_TFTP_SAST1
 enrollment url http://3.3.3.1:80
 revocation-check crl
 rsakeypair CUCME_CAPF_TFTP_SAST1 1024 1024
```

3.2.2 Creating Certificate for SAST2

Similar to creating a certificate for the different servers that was discussed in section 3.2.1; a second certificate must be created for the CTL-client. The CTL-client requires two certificates to sign the CTL file. This provides redundancy of signatures so that if one of the certificates that signed the file is revoked then the devices will use the second certificate as a backup to verify the CTL file. This configuration prevents an administrator from having to recreate and distribute the new CTL file every time a certificate is revoked.

The steps to create the second certificate (SAST2) are exactly the same as before, except the trust point will have a different name. The parameters used to create the first certificate should also be used for the second certificate. Below is a repeat of the commands that must be entered to create the second certificate.

```
crypto pki trustpoint <SAST2 trustpoint>
 enrollment url http://<IP address of CUCME>:80
 revocation-check method1
 rsakeypair <key-label> [key-size[encryption-key-size]]
 exit

crypto pki authenticate <SAST2 trustpoint>
crypto pki enroll <SAST2 trustpoint>
```

The running configuration now should show the three certificates that were created and the two certificate chains that correspond to the certificates. The three certificates should include one for the CA server, the CUCME servers, and the SAST2. Also in the configuration should be entries similar as shown below.

```
crypto pki trustpoint SAST2
 enrollment url http://3.3.3.1:80
 revocation-check crl
 rsakeypari SAST2 1024 1024
```

3.3 Configuring the Certificate Authority Proxy Function Server (CAPF)

The CAPF server is responsible for issuing Locally Significant Certificates (LSCs) and must be configured before any phone can receive an LSC. If there is not an LSC installed on the phone, then the phones can still operate securely if a Manufacturer Installed Certificate (MIC) is installed. Most of the newer phones have MICs installed, but a lot of older phones do not. Phones without a MIC can only operate securely after the LSC is installed. The following set of commands must be entered in global configuration mode.

```
capf-server
  trustpoint-label <CUCME servers' trustpoint>
  cert-enroll-trustpoint <Name of CA server> password
    [0|1] <string>
  source-addr <IP of CUCME>
  auth-mode [auth-string | LSC | MIC | none | null-string]
  cert-oper [upgrade | fetch | delete] all
  exit
```

"trustpoint-label": If a phone is configured to perform any certificate action it will try to create a Transport Layer Security (TLS) connection to the CAPF server. The trust point that is identified in this command is the certificate that will be used to create the TLS connection to the CAPF server.

"cert-enroll-trustpoint": The CAPF server must be enrolled with a CA before it will operate properly. The trust point identified in this command must be the CA's trust point. If the wrong trust point is provided then the CAPF server will not enroll the phones properly. This command requires a revocation password for the CA certificate. The password can be entered as an encrypted string or plaintext. The "0" and "1" in the command determines if the string provided is encrypted or not. The "0" represents an unencrypted string and "1" is an encrypted string.

"source-addr": This command is meant to specify the source address of the CAPF server. Even though this command specifies the IP address of the CAPF server, the CAPF server will still listen for connections on all interfaces. It is recommended that appropriate Access Control Lists (ACLs) be applied to interfaces that should not be accepting connects to the CAPF server.

"auth-mode": Before the CAPF server accepts any certificates from a phone, the phone must authenticate to the CAPF server. There are several different methods of authenticating the phones. The best practice for the authentication of phones when loading the first LSC would be to use an authorization string. Since this approach is not always feasible, the organization's security policy will dictate the best method of authentication for each of the phones. Once each phone has an LSC, the best practice is to authenticate based on a pre-existing LSC.

By default, the CAPF server will use the "none" authentication mode. The "none" option indicates that an upgrade to the certificate will not be performed. If an authorization string (auth-str) is used as the authentication method, then it is the same as having a password for each phone. When using the auth-str as the authentication method and the phone updates or deletes its certificate, the user will be prompted to enter the authorization string. The authorization string is unique per phone and must be configured as shown in section 4.2, if choosing this method of authentication. Once the string is entered correctly the phone will update or delete its certificate. The problem with this approach arises when a large number of phones exist, or the phones are located in remote locations.

For situations where there are a large number of phones or they are located remotely, the LSC, MIC, or auth-str options shown above may be used. Some phones do not come with MICs installed and the LSC may not be installed either. If the MIC is the chosen method of authentication, and is installed on all phones, then the root Cisco certificate must be enrolled with the CA. For more information on importing the root Cisco certificate, see the Cisco Unified Communications Manager Express Administration Guide.

If there are no certificates installed on the phone and entering an authentication string is too difficult, the only other option is to use a null-string. The null-string does not provide any authentication of the phones. This may be acceptable when first deploying security to a VoIP network, but other methods, such as an authorization string, should be used when managing or adding phones to the network.

"cert-oper": This is a global setting that will force the selected operation on all phones registered with the CUCME. The different options are update, fetch, and delete. The "update" command will install a new certificate if one does not already exist or replace an existing certificate. For troubleshooting purposes, the "fetch" option can be used to retrieve all of the phones certificates. The last option, "delete", is used to delete all phone certificates. This command is optional, but upon initial configuration of security on phones it is useful to upgrade all of the phones at one time.

This completes the configuration of the CAPF server and the running configuration should contain entries similar to the following.

```
capf-server
 auth-mode auth-string
 cert-enroll-trustpoint CAserver password 1 01234567891
 trustpoint-label CUCME_CAPF_TFTP_SAST1
 source-addr 3.3.3.1
```

3.4 Configuring Certificate Trust List (CTL)

The CTL-client is responsible for creating a list of all the trusted certificates, known as the CTL file. In a standard Cisco Unified Communications Manager (CUCM), there are multiple Call Managers that a device can register with. The grouping of multiple Call Managers is called a cluster. The CUCME does not support clustering, and so the CTL file will only contain the certificates for the CUCME servers that were created above.

Each time a phone that is configured for security boots, the phone will download the CTL file via TFTP and store the file on the phone. This serves as a method of downloading the certificates required to verify the TLS connection that is later made with the CUCME.

Before the CTL file can be created, the certificates for all of the servers need to be created and enrolled with the CA. After completing the procedures described in section 3.2, the following commands should be entered in the global configuration mode:

```
ctl-client
  server capf <IP address of CUCME> trustpoint <CUCME
    servers' trustpoint>
  server cme-tftp <IP address of CUCME> trustpoint <CUCME
    servers' trustpoint>
  sast1 trustpoint <CUCME servers' trustpoint>
  sast2 trustpoint <SAST2 trustpoint>
  regenerate
  exit
```

"sastX"s: The command "ctl-client" will enter into the configuration mode for the CTL-client. Once in the CTL-client's configuration mode the SAST1 and SAST2 must be identified. The SAST1 is the trust point that was created for all of the CUCME servers. The SAST2 trust point that was created earlier identifies SAST2, the back up certificate.

"server"s: The "server" commands identify the certificate that is associated with each of the servers. These commands also identify the location of the different servers. Since all of the servers are located on the router, acting as a CUCME in this example, the IP address is the local interface for the VoIP devices and the certificate will be the first certificate created in section 3.2.

The "server" command also includes a few different command options. Shown above are the "capf" and "cme-tftp" options. The "cme-tftp" option is a shortcut put in place by Cisco since the TFTP server and the CUCME is commonly on the same IP address and uses the same trustpoint. There is also the option to use them separate as "cme" and "tftp". This would give the ability to have the TFTP server located on a different server than the CUCME.

"regenerate": When configuring the CTL-client, it is important to specify the "regenerate" command when completing the configuration of this section. Without issuing this command the CTL file will not be created. In addition, the "regenerate" command will not show up in the configuration file; it is issued to create the file and is never written to the configuration file. This command must be ran any time the certificates that are used are changed. If a certificate changes and "regenerate" is not ran, then the phones will no longer trust the server that uses the updated certificate.

After configuring the CTL-client and issuing the regenerate command, there should be a file named "CTLfile.tlv" on the flash. If the CTL file is not located on the flash, then either one of the SAST certificates failed, or there was a mis-configuration of the CTL-client. The running configuration should include entries similar to the following if the CTL-client was configured properly.

```
ctl-client
  server cme-tftp 3.3.3.1 trustpoint CUCME_CAPF_TFTP_SAST1
  server capf 3.3.3.1 trustpoint CUCME_CAPF_TFTP_SAST1
  sast1 trustpoint CUCME_CAPF_TFTP_SAST1
  sast2 trustpoint SAST2
```

4 Configuring the Phone for Security Mode

After completing the previous steps, the CUCME still needs to be configured to use the correct certificates for the different functions. The functions that must be configured include the secure signaling and the TFTP authentication. The following commands must be entered in global configuration mode:

```
telephony-service
  secure-signaling trustpoint <CUCME servers' trustpoint>
  tftp-server-credentials trustpoint <CUCME servers'
truspoint>
 cnf-file perphone
exit
```

"telephony-service": This command enters the telephony service configuration mode. In this mode, global parameters can be set and the operational parameters can be set. Without the telephony service being configured, the CUCME will not be enabled.

"secure-signaling": To provide security of the call signaling, the CUCME must be configured to use a certificate for any TLS connections that are initiated with it. The "secure-signaling" command also identifies the trust point that will be used for any TLS connections.

"tftp-server-credentials": The TFTP server must sign all files that the phones will download. These files also include all of the phones configuration files. Before the TFTP server can sign any of the files, the TFTP server must be configured to use the appropriate certificate for signing.

"cnf-file perphone": The CNF file is the configuration file that the phones use. Enabling security requires that each phone have an individual CNF file. The CUCME cannot use a generic configuration file and change the name of the file on the fly because of the signing issues.

Once the foundation of the CUCME is configured to support security, the next step is to configure the phones for security mode. There are two methods for configuring the phones for security mode. Those two methods are:

- Configure the global device security mode for supported phone models.
- Configure the device security mode for a single device.

The following section provides instructions on how to set global device security mode and single device methods.

When the IP phone is configured for authentication, the CUCME service provides integrity and authentication for the phone using TLS connection for call signaling, without encrypting the voice media. When the IP phone is configured for encryption, the CUCME service provides integrity, authentication, and confidentiality using TLS connection for the call signaling, and AES128/SHA encryption for the voice media.

4.1 Global Device Security Mode

In the CUCME router, the default setting of the global device security mode for all phone types is "none", which means the phones are in a Non-Secure mode. To change the setting in the telephone-service global parameters to authenticated or encrypted, perform the following steps in global configuration mode:

```
telephony-service
  device-security-mode [authenticated | encrypted | none]
  load-cfg-file <file-url> alias <file-alias> [sign] [create]
  reset all
```

"device-security-mode": Inside the telephony service configuration mode, this command can be entered to apply enterprise wide changes to the phones. The "authenticated" option will configure all phones to establish a TLS connection for the call signaling, but the voice media will remain unencrypted. The "encrypted" option creates the TLS connection for call signaling, and also encrypts the voice media. Using the "none" option does not provide any security for the call signaling or the voice media. It is recommended that the "encrypted" option is used to provide the highest level of assurance.

"load-cfg-file" (optional): Once security is enabled on the phone, the phones will no longer accept unsigned files from the TFTP server. To allow for the TFTP server to serve out pre-existing files or files not created by the CUCME, they must be signed. This load-cfg-file command will perform that function. The "file-url" is the exact location of the file, and the "file-alias" is simply the name that the TFTP server will use. The first time that this command is used for each file, the "create" keyword in addition to the "sign" keyword should be used. This allows for the file to be signed and a signed version of the file to be created.

At this point in the configuration, the phones can be reset and should begin connecting securely. The phones will not register securely until a certificate exists on the phone. This means that any phones without a certificate installed must have a pending certificate operation. To reset all of the phones in the network, the "reset all" command can be run inside the telephony service configuration mode. The running configuration file should now contain entries similar to the following:

```
telephony-service
  secure-signaling trustpoint CUCME_CAPF_TFTP_SAST1
  cnf-perphone
  tftp-server-credentials trustpoint CUCME_CAPF_TFTP_SAST1
  device-security-mode encrypted
  load-cfg-file flash:Ringlist.xml alias Ringlist.xml sign
```

4.2 Security Mode for a Single Device

Depending on the deployment environment it may be necessary to apply different levels of security to specific devices. The following section will provide the steps to apply different levels of security to individual devices. It should be noted that if global security parameters were set using section 4.1, then the following procedures would override those settings. This allows for the default configuration to have one security level and specific phones be configured for another security level.

For each phone the following commands can be entered to enable the desired level of security. The following series of commands must be entered in the global configuration mode:

```
ephone <phone-label>
 mac-address CAFÉ.CAFE.1234
device-security-mode [authenticated | encrypted | none]
 capf-auth-str <digit-string>
 cert-oper [upgrade | fetch | delete] auth-mode [auth-
string | LSC | MIC | none | null-string]
 reset
```

"ephone": During the initial CUCME configuration, there are several options as to how many phones the CUCME will allow to register and if auto-registration is accepted. Once the number of ephones is configured, the CUCME will generate entries in the configurations file for the desired number of phones. These entries are very similar to interfaces that exist on a router. If auto-registration is enabled and a MAC address is not assigned to the ephone, the phone labels will be almost meaningless because the phones will be assigned to the first available ephone. This creates a problem when attempting to assign specific phones a different level of security from the rest. To solve this problem it is suggested that auto-registration be disabled and MAC addresses assigned to each phone label. Auto-registration should also be disabled for security reasons. This allows for the phone label of the ephone to uniquely identify a specific phone.

"device-security-mode": Inside the desired ephone configuration mode, this command will override any global security levels and enforce the selected security level. The "authenticated" option will configure all phones to establish a TLS connection for the call signaling, but the voice media will remain unencrypted. The "encrypted" option creates the TLS connection for call signaling, and encrypts the voice media. Using the "none" option does not provide any security.

"capf-auth-str" (optional): This command is only required if an authentication string is the chosen authentication method for either the global CAPF server or for the phone.

13

This command will assign a specific authentication string to the selected phone. The CAPF server can also assign global authentication strings; however, this is not recommended because it is not a secure method of authenticating the phones.

"cert-oper" (optional): This command applies the selected operation on the individual phone. It is useful in the case when an individual phone's certificate needs to be upgraded or debugged. This command is slightly different from the "cert-oper" that is used in the CAPF server configuration. This command requires the operation that should be taken followed by the authentication mode. It is recommended to use either an authorization string or a pre-existing LSC if available for the authorization mode.

"reset": This command will reset the individual phone, but only works when the phone is registered to the CUCME. If the phone is not registered, then the phone will not respond to the "reset" command.

After entering these commands and resetting the individual phone, then it will be configured for encryption. Once again, the phone must have a certificate installed before creating a TLS session with the CUCME. If a certificate is not installed, then a pending certificate operation with the CAPF must be configured. Using this method, each phone must be configured individually. The running configuration should show entries similar to the following. Note that the "cert-oper" will only appear while there is an operation pending. Once the operation has completed, the command will be removed from the running configuration.

```
telephony-service
 secure-signaling trustpoint CUCME_CAPF_TFTP_SAST1
 cnf-perphone
 tftp-server-credentials trustpoint CUCME_CAPF_TFTP_SAST1
 !
ephone 1
 mac-address CAFE.CAFE.1234
 device-security-mode encrypted
 !
ephone 2
 mac-address CAFE.CAFE.1235
 device-security-mode authenticated
 capf-auth-string 1234
```

5 Hardening the Phone

To further tighten security on the phone, the following settings are recommended:

- Disabling Gratuitous Address Resolution Protocol (GARP)
- Disabling Web Access
- Disabling PC Voice VLAN Access
- Disabling Settings Access
- Disabling PC Port
- Disabling Speaker and Headset

Disable the Gratuitous Address Resolution Protocol (GARP)***:*** Gratuitous ARP is when the Cisco IP Phone receives an unsolicited ARP reply, that is an ARP reply when the phone did not send a request, then uses this unsolicited ARP reply to update its ARP table. By doing so, it is possible to spoof a valid network device. Gratuitous ARP is enabled by default on Cisco IP Phones.

Disable Web Access: When Web Access is disabled, the phone will block HTTP port 80. With this setting disabled, users will not be able to access the phone's internal web pages to view statistic and configuration information. The phone's HTTP server is enabled by default.

Disable PC Voice VLAN Access: The default factory setting for Cisco IP phones is to forward all packets that are received from the network switch to the PC port. When this setting is set to "disabled" a PC connected to the PC port will not be able to sniff the traffic coming to the phone that is VLAN tagged.

Note: Cisco IP Phone models 7940 and 7960 will drop any packets tagged with the voice VLAN. Cisco IP Phone model 7970 will drop any packet that contains any 802.1Q tag on any VLAN.

Disable Settings Access: This capability setting enables a user to access information about their phone (e.g., network configuration, user settings, and model information) via the keypad. The three options for this field are Enabled, Disabled, and Restricted. When the "Disabled" option is selected, configuration settings and network information will not be viewable by local users. When the "Restricted" option is selected, only user preferences and volume settings can be modified on the phone display.

Disable PC Port: By default, the PC port on all Cisco IP phones that have a PC port is enabled. A primary example of usage of the PC port from a user perspective is when the user only has one Ethernet drop. A computer can be connected through the IP Phone PC port for connectivity to the network. If this feature is enabled, it becomes imperative to have the PC Voice VLAN Access set to disabled.

Disable Speaker and Headset: A majority of the Cisco IP phones have a speakerphone and a headset connection. All of these connections are enabled by default. At the 2007 Hack.lu conference, several of the Cisco 7900 series phones were identified as vulnerable to eavesdropping attacks. To prevent eavesdropping, it is necessary to disable the speakerphone and headset.

In general, there are two methods for hardening the phones. The first method is to set the device parameters at the global level. The second method is to harden the phones individually. The following sections provide instructions for both the global level and individual phone hardening methods.

5.1 Global Phone Hardening

The following commands can be used to apply the desired level of security to all phones that are registered to the CUCME. Each of these commands must be entered in the global configuration mode.

```
telephony-service
  service phone disableSpeaker true
  service phone disableSpeakerAndHeadset true
  service phone forwardingDelay 1
  service phone garp 1
  service phone pcPort 1
  service phone spanToPCPort 1
  service phone voiceVlanAccess 1
  service phone webAccess 1
  service phone settingsAccess 2
create cnf-files
reset all
```

"service phone": The service phone command allows for individual XML fields from the phone's configuration file to be modified. The parameters for this command are the XML field name followed by the value of the field. Almost all of the vendor configuration fields can be modified. The parameters and values shown above are the recommended minimum for hardening the IP phones. For a complete list of fields and their values, refer to http://www.cisco.com/en/US/docs/voice_ip_comm/cucme/ command/reference/cme_s1ht.html. The following contains the XML fields shown above with a description of their parameters. Some of the parameters from Cisco's documentation were found to be inconsistent with testing that was performed. The "disableSpeaker", "disableSpeakerAndHeadset", and "garp" parameters have been changed from Cisco's documentation to reflect the results of testing. It should be noted that all parameters are case sensitive.

Table 1: Cisco's description of each parameter shown above

Parameter	Description
disableSpeaker {true | false}	Enables and disables the speakerphone ■ True – Speakerphone disabled ■ False – Speakerphone enabled (default)
disableSpeakerAndHeadset {true | false}	Enables and disables the speakerphone and headset ■ True – Speakerphone and headset disabled ■ False – Speakerphone and headset enabled (default)
forwardingDelay {0 | 1}	Enables and disables the activation of the IP phone's PC Ethernet switch port when the IP phone boots to prevent Ethernet traffic from interfering with the bootup process. ■ 0 – Disabled ■ 1 – Enabled (default)
garp {0 | 1}	Enable and disables IP phone response to gratuitous Address Resolution Protocol (ARP) messages from the IP phone's Ethernet interface ■ 0 – Garp enabled (default) ■ 1 – Garp disabled
pcPort {0 | 1}	Enables and disables the Ethernet switch port on the phone

	so the IP phone can have access to an Ethernet connection for a PC connection through the phone. • 0 – Enabled (default) • 1 – Disabled
spanToPCPort {0 | 1}	Enables and disables the path between the Ethernet switch port of an IP phone and a connection to a PC. • 0 – Enabled (default) • 1 – Disabled
voiceVlanAccess {0 | 1}	Enables and disables spanning, which is the IP phone's access to the voice VLAN of the PC to which the IP phone's Ethernet port is connected. • 0 – Enabled (default) • 1 – Disabled **Note** For Cisco Unified IP Phone 7985, the default is Disabled (1)
webAccess {0 | 1 | 2}	Enable and disables web access that allows phone users to configure settings and features on User Option web pages. • 0 – Enabled (default) • 1 – Disabled • 2 – Read Only. For the Cisco Unified IP Phone 7921G only. The phone user can view only User Option web pages and cannot modify settings and features on the pages **Note** For the Cisco Unified IP Phone 7921G , the default is Read Only (2)
settingsAccess {0 | 1 | 2}	Enables and disables the Settings button on an IP phone. • 0 – Disabled • 1 – Enabled (default). The phone user can modify features by using the Settings menu. • 2 – Restricted. The phone user is allowed to access User Preferences and volume settings only.

"create cnf-files": After changes have been made to the telephony service configuration, the phone's XML configuration files must be updated. Issuing this command in the telephony service configuration mode will regenerate all of the configuration files for all phones that are currently registered. These settings will not take affect until the phones are reset. To reset all registered devices at the same time, issue the "reset all" command in the telephony service configuration mode.

After following the instructions above and resetting all of the devices registered with the CUCME, the changes will have taken effect. The running configuration should contain entries similar to below:

```
telephony-service
 service phone disableSpeaker true
 service phone disableSpeakerAndHeadset true
 service phone forwardingDelay 1
 service phone garp 1
 service phone pcPort 1
 service phone spanToPCPort 1
 service phone voiceVlanAccess 1
 service phone webAccess 1
 service phone settingsAccess 2
```

5.2 Individual Phone Hardening

Phones may be placed at various locations throughout the enterprise, eg. some in public spaces and some within protected spaces. Phones located in public spaces should be configured to deny any attempt to access the phone's settings. Phones located in protected spaces may be configured to allow a user to access and modified a limited set of settings. Cisco has provided the ability to configure individual settings for each phone by creating ephone-templates. Each template may contain different settings and may be applied to one or more phones creating different classes of phones. To harden the IP phones using the individual phone method, the following steps from the global configuration mode should be performed:

```
ephone-template <template label>
 service phone disableSpeaker true
 service phone disableSpeakerAndHeadset true
 service phone forwardingDelay 1
 service phone garp 1
 service phone pcPort 1
 service phone spanToPCPort 1
 service phone voiceVlanAccess 1
 service phone webAccess 1
 service phone settingsAccess 2
 exit
ephone <ephone label>
 ephone-template <template label>
 exit
telephony-service
 create cnf-files
 exit
ephone <ephone label>
 reset
```

"ephone-template": This command creates a new template with the user defined label. Inside this template several options for the phones can be configured. Above, several "service phone" commands are set with different values that apply to a phone's XML configuration file. The values for each parameter shown above are the recommended values for hardening a phone. These values may have to be adjusted to fit each individual environment. For further explanation of the phone parameters that are shown above, refer to Table 1.

"ephone": Once the ephone template is configured the template must be applied to each device that it pertains to. The "ephone" command followed by the label of the desired device, will place the router in the selected ephone's configuration.

"ephone-template": Though the syntax is exactly the same as before, this command has a completely different meaning now that the router is in the ephone's configuration mode. When entered in the ephone configuration mode, this command will apply any settings that were configured in the ephone template, to the selected device. This process must be completed for each device that will have an ephone template associated with it.

"create cnf-files": After applying all templates to the desired devices, the changes will not take effect until the configuration files are updated. To update the configuration files, the "create cnf-files" command has to be issued. This command is entered in the telephony service configuration mode. The command will recreate all configuration files for all devices and apply any changes that have been made since the last creation of the configuration files.

"reset": The reset command can be issued for each device by entering it in each device ephone configuration or all devices can be reset at one time by issuing a "reset all" in the telephony service configuration mode.

Once the phones have been issued the reset all command, the hardening procedures should be effective. This completes the phone hardening procedures. If all of the steps described in this document were followed, the CUCME and all associated devices will be configured for authentication, security, and hardened. An example of a configuration that applies all of these methods can be found in Appendix B and C.

Appendix A: Definition of terminologies extracted from Cisco documentation

Term	Definition
Authentication	Process that verifies the identity of an entity.
Advanced Encrypted Standard (AES)	AES is a symmetric key encryption algorithm and is adopted by the U.S. Government, Department of Defense, and private industry world wide for data encryption.
Certificate Authority Proxy Function (CAPF)	Process whereby supported devices can request locally significant certificates by using CUCME Administration.
Certificate Trust List (CTL)	List that Cisco IP Phones use; a file that you create after you install and configure the Cisco CTL client in the CUCME; contains a predefined list of trusted certificates that the Cisco Site Administrator Security Token signs; provides authentication information to validate the certificates for servers.
Site Administrator Security Token (SAST)	Can be a portable hardware security module that contains a private key and an X.509v3 certificate that the Cisco Certificate Authority signs, but normally found with a CUCM. CUCME uses a X.509v3 certificate and RSA key pair generated by a Cisco IOS CA or other third party CA. The x.509v3 certificate and RSA keys are used for signing the CTL file.
Device Authentication	Process that validates the identity of the device and ensures that the entity is what it claims to be.
Encryption	Process that ensures that only the intended recipient receives and reads the data; process that ensures the confidentiality of the information; process that translates data into cipher text, which appears random and meaningless.
File Authentication	Process that validates digitally signed files that the phone downloads. The phone validates the signature to make sure that file tampering did not occur after the file creation.
Image Authentication	Process that prevents tampering with the binary image prior to loading it on the phone; process whereby a phone validates the integrity and source of an image.
Transport Layer Security (TLS)	A security protocol defined by the IETF; that provides integrity, authentication, and encryption and resides in the TCP layer in the IP communications stack.
Integrity	Process that ensures that data tampering has not occurred between entities.
Locally Significant Certification (LSC)	A digital x.509v3 certificate that is installed on the phone; issued by a certificate authority using CAPF server. This certificate is used as the primary certificate for encrypting the phones transmissions. This certificate takes priority over a MIC.

Media Encryption	Process whereby the confidentiality of the media occurs by using cryptographic procedures. Media encryption uses the Secure Real Time Protocol (SRTP) as defined in IETF RFC 3711.
Manufacture Installed Certificate (MIC)	A digital x.509v3 certificate that is signed by the Cisco Certificate authority and installed in supported phones by Cisco Manufacturing. This certificate can be used for encrypting the phones transmission if there exist no LSC.
Trivial File Transfer Protocol (TFTP)	A simple file transfer protocol used by the phones to get its setting from the CCM server or TFTP server.
Non-secure Call	Call in which at least one device is not authenticated or encrypted.
Secure Call	Call in which all devices are authenticated, and the media stream is encrypted.
Signaling Authentication	Process that validates that no tampering occurred to signaling packets during transmission; uses the Transport Layer Security protocol.
Signaling Encryption	Process that uses cryptographic methods to protect the confidentiality of all SCCP signaling messages that are sent between the device and the Cisco CallManager server.

Appendix B: Secure CUCME with Global Phone Settings

```
ctl-client
 server cme-tftp 1.2.3.4 trustpoint CUCME_CAPF_TFTP_SAST1
 server capf 1.2.3.4 trustpoint CUCME_CAPF_TFTP_SAST1
 sast1 trustpoint CUCME_CAPF_TFTP_SAST1
 sast2 trustpoint SAST2
!
capf-server
 port 3804
 auth-mode auth-str
 cert-enroll-trustpoint CAServer password 1 03085A090A0E23404F0B
 trustpoint-label CUCME_CAPF_TFTP_SAST1
 source-addr 1.2.3.4
!
crypto pki server CAServer
 database level complete
 grant auto
 database url flash:/
!
crypto pki trustpoint CAServer
 enrollment url http://1.2.3.4:80
 revocation-check crl
 rsakeypair CMEServer
!
crypto pki trustpoint CUCME_CAPF_TFTP_SAST1
 enrollment url http://1.2.3.4:80
 serial-number
 revocation-check crl
 rsakeypair CUCME_CAPF_TFTP_SAST1 1024 1024
!
crypto pki trustpoint SAST2
 enrollment url http://1.2.3.4:80
 serial-number
 revocation-check crl
 rsakeypair CUCME_CAPF_TFTP_SAST1 1024 1024
!
crypto pki certificate chain CAServer
 certificate ca 01
  ...
     quit
crypto pki certificate chain CUCME_CAPF_TFTP_SAST1
 certificate 02
  ...
     quit
 certificate ca 01
  ...
     quit
crypto pki certificate chain SAST2
 certificate 03
  ...
     quit
 certificate ca 01
  ...
     quit
```

```
!
interface FastEthernet0/3/4
 switchport voice vlan 10
!
interface FastEthernet0/3/7
 switchport voice vlan 10
!
interface Vlan10
 ip address 1.2.3.4 255.255.255.0
!
ip http server
!
telephony-service
 max-ephones 4
 max-dn 4
 ip source-address 1.2.3.4 port 2000
 secure-signaling trustpoint CUCME_CAPF_TFTP_SAST1
 service phone disableSpeaker true
 service phone disableSpeakerAndHeadset true
 service phone forwardingDelay 1
 service phone garp 1
 service phone pcPort 1
 service phone spanToPCPort 1
 service phone voiceVlanAccess 0
 service phone webAccess 1
 service phone settingsAccess 2
 secure-signaling trustpoint CME
 cnf-file perphone
 dialplan-pattern 1 27... extension-length 4
 tftp-server-credentials trustpoint CUCME_CAPF_TFTP_SAST1
 server-security-mode secure
 device-security-mode encrypted
 load-cfg-file flash:P00308000500.sbn alias P00308000500.sbn sign
 load-cfg-file flash:P00308000500.sb2 alias P00308000500.sb2 sign
 load-cfg-file flash:P00308000500.loads alias P00308000500.loads sign
 create cnf-files version-stamp Jan 01 2002 00:00:00
!
ephone-dn  1
 number 7001
!
ephone-dn  2
 number 7002
!
ephone-dn  3
 number 7003
!
ephone-dn 4
 number 7004
!
ephone  1
 device-security-mode encrypted
 mac-address CAFE.CAFE.1234
 type 7970
 button  1:1
!
ephone  2
 device-security-mode encrypted
```

```
 mac-address CAFE.CAFE.2345
 button  1:2
!
ephone  3
 device-security-mode encrypted
 mac-address CAFE.CAFE.3456
 button  1:3
!
ephone  4
 device-security-mode encrypted
 mac-address CAFE.CAFE.4567
 button  1:4
```

Appendix C: Secure CUCME with Individual Settings

```
ctl-client
 server cme-tftp 1.2.3.4 trustpoint CUCME_CAPF_TFTP_SAST1
 server capf 1.2.3.4 trustpoint CUCME_CAPF_TFTP_SAST1
 sast1 trustpoint CUCME_CAPF_TFTP_SAST1
 sast2 trustpoint SAST2
!
capf-server
 port 3804
 auth-mode auth-str
 cert-enroll-trustpoint CAServer password 1 03085A090A0E23404F0B
 trustpoint-label CUCME_CAPF_TFTP_SAST1
 source-addr 1.2.3.4
!
crypto pki server CAServer
 database level complete
 grant auto
 database url flash:/
!
crypto pki trustpoint CAServer
 enrollment url http://1.2.3.4:80
 revocation-check crl
 rsakeypair CMEServer
!
crypto pki trustpoint CUCME_CAPF_TFTP_SAST1
 enrollment url http://1.2.3.4:80
 serial-number
 revocation-check crl
 rsakeypair CUCME_CAPF_TFTP_SAST1 1024 1024
!
crypto pki trustpoint SAST2
 enrollment url http://1.2.3.4:80
 serial-number
 revocation-check crl
 rsakeypair CUCME_CAPF_TFTP_SAST1 1024 1024
!
crypto pki certificate chain CAServer
 certificate ca 01
  ...
     quit
crypto pki certificate chain CUCME_CAPF_TFTP_SAST1
 certificate 02
  ...
     quit
 certificate ca 01
  ...
     quit
crypto pki certificate chain SAST2
 certificate 03
  ...
     quit
 certificate ca 01
  ...
     quit
!
```

```
interface FastEthernet0/3/4
 switchport voice vlan 10
!
interface FastEthernet0/3/7
 switchport voice vlan 10
!
interface Vlan10
 ip address 1.2.3.4 255.255.255.0
!
ip http server
!
telephony-service
 max-ephones 4
 max-dn 4
 ip source-address 1.2.3.4 port 2000
 secure-signaling trustpoint CUCME_CAPF_TFTP_SAST1
 cnf-file perphone
 dialplan-pattern 1 27... extension-length 4
 tftp-server-credentials trustpoint CUCME_CAPF_TFTP_SAST1
 server-security-mode secure
 device-security-mode encrypted
 load-cfg-file flash:P00308000500.sbn alias P00308000500.sbn sign
 load-cfg-file flash:P00308000500.sb2 alias P00308000500.sb2 sign
 load-cfg-file flash:P00308000500.loads alias P00308000500.loads
sign
 create cnf-files version-stamp Jan 01 2002 00:00:00
!
ephone-template  1
 service phone disableSpeaker true
 service phone disableSpeakerAndHeadset true
 service phone forwardingDelay 1
 service phone garp 1
 service phone pcPort 1
 service phone spanToPCPort 1
 service phone voiceVlanAccess 1
 service phone webAccess 1
 service phone settingsAccess 1
!
ephone-template  2
 service phone disableSpeaker true
 service phone disableSpeakerAndHeadset true
 service phone forwardingDelay 1
 service phone garp 1
 service phone pcPort 1
 service phone spanToPCPort 1
 service phone voiceVlanAccess 1
 service phone webAccess 1
 service phone settingsAccess 0
!
ephone-dn  1
 number 7001
!
ephone-dn  2
 number 7002
!
ephone-dn  3
 number 7003
```

```
!
ephone-dn 4
 number 7004
!
ephone  1
 device-security-mode encrypted
 mac-address CAFE.CAFE.1234
 ephone-template 1
 button  1:1
!
ephone  2
 device-security-mode authenticated
 mac-address CAFE.CAFE.2345
 ephone-template 2
 button  1:2
!
ephone  3
 device-security-mode encrypted
 mac-address CAFE.CAFE.3456
 ephone-template 2
 button  1:3
!
ephone  4
 device-security-mode encrypted
 mac-address CAFE.CAFE.4567
 ephone-template 2
 button  1:4
```

References

Additional information on this topic can be found in the following documents:

Cisco, *Configuring (CME) Security* from *Cisco Unified Communications Manager Express System Administrator Guide*, document # OL-106663-02, http://www.cisco.com/en/US/docs/voice_ip_comm/cucme/admin/configuration/guide/cmead.pdf, November 2007.

NSA, *Security Guidance for Deploying IP Telephony Systems*, version 1.01, Report Number I332-016R-2005, http://www.nsa.gov/snac/voip/I332-016R-2005.PDF, February 2006.

Follett, Jennifer, *Security Flaw Opens Cisco VoIP Phones to Eavesdropping*, ChannelWeb, www.crn.com/networking/204301121, November 2007.